Daniel and the Lions' Den

Copyright © 1993 by Hunt & Thorpe

Published in Nashville, Tennessee, by Oliver-Nelson Books, a
division of Thomas Nelson, Inc., Publishers, and distributed in
Canada by Lawson Falle, Ltd., Cambridge, Ontario.

Printed in Malaysia

Library of Congress Cataloging-in-Publication Data

Pipe, Rhona.
Daniel and the lions' den/Rhona Pipe; illustrated by Annabel Spencely.
p. cm. — (Now I can read Bible stories)
Summary: A simple retelling of the Bible story in which Daniel is
thrown into the lions' den and is saved by God.
ISBN 0-8407-3422-0
1. Daniel (Biblical character) — Juvenile literature. 2. Bible
stories, English — O.T. Daniel. [1. Daniel (Biblical character)
2. Bible stories — O.T.]. I. Spencely, Annabel. ill. II. Title.
III. Series.
BS580-D2P56 1992
224'.509505 — dc20

92-12073
CIP
AC

1 2 3 4 5 6 — 98 97 96 95 94 93

Daniel and the Lions' Den

Rhona Pipe

Illustrated by
Annabel Spenceley

OLIVER
NELSON

THOMAS NELSON PUBLISHERS
Nashville

"Daniel is the best man I have,"
said the king.
"I trust him.
I will make him my
prime minister."

This made the top men
in the kingdom mad.

"We do not want Daniel to boss us," they said.
"It is time to get rid of him.
Make a list of all the
bad things he does.
Give the list to the king."
Did the plan work? No!
Daniel did not do bad things.
"We will try plan B,"
they said.

The top men went to the king.
"O great king," they said.
"O king, may you live a long time.
Make a law that people must pray
only to you.
Anyone who breaks the law
will be thrown to the lions."
"What a good idea!"
the king said.

As soon as the law was passed,
Daniel went home.
He went upstairs and prayed to God.
He prayed by the window
as he always did.

The top men rushed to the king.
"O great king," they said.
"What a bad thing!
Daniel is praying.
And not to you!
To the lions with him!"
Then the king saw that he
had been tricked.
But it was too late.

All day long the king
did his best to think.
He tried to find a way
to save Daniel.
At the end of the day
the top men came back.
"You cannot break one
of your own laws,"
they said.
"Very well," said the king.
"Take Daniel to the lions' pit."

The king went to see Daniel.

"I am sorry," he said.

"Maybe your God will save you."

They let Daniel down into the pit full of lions.

They put a stone over the mouth of the pit.

The stone had the king's seal.

The king went back to
his palace.
He was too upset
to eat or drink.
He stayed awake all night.
He thought about the lions
and Daniel.

When the sun came up,
the king went to the pit.
"Daniel," he called.
"Has your God saved you?"
And Daniel called back,
"O king, may you live a long time.
My God sent an angel.
The angel closed the mouths
of the lions.
I am not hurt at all."

The king was happy.
"Pull Daniel out!" he said.
"And throw all my top men in."
Then the king sent out a letter.
It said: Daniel's God is the true God.
He is a God who saves those
who trust Him.
I am making a new law.
Everyone is to pray to Daniel's God.